DEVOURED BY
CANNABIS

DEVOURED BY CANNABIS

Weed, Liberty, and Legalization

DOUGLAS WILSON

canonpress

moscow, idaho | www.canonpress.com

Published by Canon Press
P.O. Box 8729, Moscow, Idaho 83843
800.488.2034 | www.canonpress.com

Cover design and interior layout by James Engerbretson.

Printed in the United States of America.

Unless otherwise indicated, Scripture quotations are from the King James Version. Bible quotations marked NKJV are from the New King James Version®. Copyright ©1982 by Thomas Nelson, Inc. Used by permission. All rights reserved. Bible quotations marked NIV are from the New International Version®. Copyright © 1973, 1978, 1984, 2011 by Biblica, Inc.® Used by permission. All rights reserved worldwide.

Library of Congress Cataloging-in-Publication Data forthcoming

21 22 23 24 25 26 27   10 9 8 7 6 5 4 3 2

This book is for Peter Hitchens.

CONTENTS

THE CONDITION OUR CONDITION IS IN

The complete legalization of marijuana seems like an idea whose time has come. As I write these words, the recreational use of marijuana is legal in twelve states, and medical marijuana is now accepted in thirty-four states. The drug remains against the law at the federal level, but there doesn't seem to be any real interest at all in strict enforcement. For many observers, it seems that legalization at the federal level is only a matter of time.

In addition, this movement toward legal status has been paralleled by a great increase in social and cultural acceptance. Nobody wants to be seen as buying into any throwback *Reefer Madness* frenzy. Opposition to legal weed is now quite easily represented as the hidebound opinions of mindless traditionalists. In addition, these traditionalists, many of whom enjoy a good martini, are characterized as inconsistent and hypocritical. They have for some reason drawn an arbitrary line against someone *else's* kicks.

So marijuana has been around in a markedly public way for a generation now. But this has been in its own way a contributor to some significant misunderstanding. We think we have been dealing with the same drug all this time, but in a fundamental way, that is not exactly true.

The active ingredient in marijuana is THC (delta-9-tetrahydrocannabinol), and the toxicity of a Woodstock joint was relatively low—a modest amount of THC. Today the levels can get a *lot* higher, just like the user. And there are a number of people who are now using extracts that are almost entirely pure THC. Whatever kick that mule had back in the seventies, it is about four to six times greater than that now. This is kind of like the difference between a Bud Light and a shot of Old Gym Sock Corn Whiskey. Sure, there is alcohol in both, but still . . .

Also, in the seventies, it was common for people to say they were "experimenting" with drugs. And individuals *were* experimenting with them, and our culture as a whole was experimenting with them. But we are in quite a different place now, and we have enough data to be able to say that the experiment has already been run. We have had a generation or more of widespread drug use. If we are willing to look at the results, the results are actually in.

Tens of thousands have participated in this *ad hoc* research project, and plenty of research has been done. There were many volunteers. The results are now gathered, and I hope to point to some of the results of this *ad hoc* research later in this book. Though the culture-wide experiment was somewhat loose, a number of rigorous studies have been conducted on various subsets within that broader culture.

Nevertheless, despite the obvious and predictable outcome, these results are largely being ignored. Many know what they would *like* the truth to be, but they have been more influenced by a pro-marijuana lobbying effort than they recognize. In the battles for establishing medical marijuana and for legalizing recreational marijuana, the monetary investment of the pro-pot forces has been massive. The worshipers of Mammon have known for a long time that there is big money to be made from large numbers of people who have acquired a bad habit. There's gold in them thar potheads.

Not only so, but a number of overreaching politicians seem to have figured out that they might have a significantly easier time governing a nation of lotus eaters than a nation of energetic and freedom-loving citizens. In addition, given the rise in the popularity of socialism, it would make sense to legalize and popularize the use of marijuana. Socialists need a populace that is capable of following their economic arguments.

And speaking of a change of sentiment, the last few years have seen an astonishing reversal. Just a few years ago, people selling pot were the drug dealers, and people administering the miracles generated by the pharmaceutical companies were healers. As Darren Doane has pointed out, because *brand* is far more powerful than approved-establishment-think, the whole situation has flipped.[1] Big Pharma is now the baddie, selling ugly colored pills in plastic bottles, and the cannabis dealers are looking fair to usher us all back into the Summer of Love, 1967-style.

What are some of the results I mentioned earlier? States that legalized recreational marijuana were promised an economic bonanza. There would be *beaucoup* tax revenues from the sale of legalized pot. There would be reduced costs when it came to drug enforcement, and prison costs would obviously go down as well. There would be fluffy white clouds in the sky, and possibly unicorns. Not only have these promises failed to materialize, there have also been some other surprises.

Employers who want a labor pool that is not made up of stoners have had to to relocate to another state in order to find that kind of labor pool. If you run a

1. Darren Doane, "What Cannabis Gets Right and Big Pharma Gets Wrong," LinkedIn, September 2, 2019: https://www.linkedin.com/pulse/what-canna-bis-gets-right-big-pharma-wrong-darren-doane/?fbclid=IwAR18E3y7RfvYWx-gVW9dS7gWjIVz7psy1dcnEzz9-HHMxbqC1yuG-C_tka9Y.

business that uses heavy equipment (say, oil drilling), you do not want people with THC in their systems to be anywhere near that equipment—for both safety and liability reasons.[2] The problems with alcohol abuse on the part of employees *can* be similar, but at the same time they are significantly different. The half life of alcohol in the body's system is short. A pint of beer takes about two hours to metabolize. THC stays in the system for days.

On top of that, there is a correlation between significant pot use and psychosis. There is some debate over whether pot can cause schizophrenia, or whether it is a substance that can simply accelerate the problem for those who were already predisposed to schizophrenia. In either case, that is not what should be described as a good trend. Whether the drug drives people to the cliff and throws them over, or if it merely pushes off the people who were already standing there, the issue should be a matter of concern either way.

This link between pot use and crazy has been known for quite a while, even if it has been overstated at times (as in, *Reefer Madness*). This is not really disputed unless the game being played is overtly political. Some of our newly legal cannabis stores will actually label some varieties of pot as *less* likely to cause paranoia. So what does that make the other *unlabeled* varieties? Can anyone say *more* likely?

2. Patrick James, "Colorado Businessman Blames 'Stoned' Workers for Move to SC," Noozsaurus.com, April 25, 2015: http://www.noozsaurus.com/colorado-businessman-blames-stoned-workers-move-sc/.

To make matters worse, there is also a relationship between such psychosis and violence. When the crime is both irrational and spectacular (such as a father coming unhinged and killing his family), and the tragedy is the result of a psychotic episode, it is really *not* unreasonable to ask if weed was a factor.

One of the questions we *ought* to ask whenever there is an episode of inexplicable violence (school shooting, etc.) is whether or not there were any drugs in the shooter's system. It is easy to pinpoint what kind of gun was used, and then to yell about guns for a while, and whether the troubled student was wearing a black overcoat, but none of this is helpful.

And there are some *other* factors with possible relevance. How many of the more recent mass shooters were young men who grew up without a father? How many of them were on medications prescribed by a doctor and administered by the school nurse? How many of them were supplementing these legal drugs with their own drugs, most notably pot? And returning to the first point, how many of these unfortunate souls were using drugs in the first place because they had grown up without a dad? In short, perhaps toxic masculinity is the result of an absent masculinity, by which I mean the father being elsewhere.

In addition to all of this, you have the run-of-the-mill petty crimes that are going to be plentiful when people in poverty have a ravenous habit or addiction. Often that habit is what reduced them to impoverished circumstances in the first place, but the internal demands do not go away just because the money is gone. And this leads to problems like theft as a simple means of affording the needed drugs.

As will become apparent in the first few chapters, I am writing for Christians who accept the authority of Scripture, at least in principle. This is because the widespread acceptance of pot smoking in the world has had a significant impact on the Christian world in ways that it shouldn't have, and I believe that we believers need to get our thinking straight "in-house" before we attempt to say anything to the outside world.

Another point should be made before we begin. Although this is a book on marijuana, we will be looking at many scriptural passages that address alcohol use. This is not because they are the same kind of thing, but rather because they are generally *perceived* as being the same kind of thing. This is a false analogy that has created quite a bit of confusion, and so we will spend some time disentangling these two issues.

Although our culture appears to be pursuing the wide-spread acceptance and legalization of marijuana use, blowing through one green light after another, I hope that this small book occasions *some* second thoughts. And even if we cannot get the red light that I would wish (and will be arguing for later on), perhaps we can at least work our way to a flashing yellow one.

CHAPTER ONE

IS MARIJUANA LIKE ALCOHOL?

O ne of the stumbling blocks for Christians is that they don't know all that much about marijuana, but they do live in a Christian culture that has largely (but fairly recently) accepted the moderate drinking of alcohol. The old-time evangelicalism of their great-grandparents was as dry as Ezekiel's valley of bones, but those days are now clearly in the rearview mirror.

Alcohol has been newly accepted, so is it now time for us to unbend just a little bit more? Perhaps we should do with marijuana what a previous generation did with beer and wine.

Maybe this is simply a generational divide. One generation likes a dry martini after work, and a new generation prefers a smoky kick. Couldn't it just be a matter of generational taste? One prefers a smoky kick with actual smoke, while the other wants the smoky kick of Laphroaig, which, as the ad copy once put it, "tastes like a burning hospital."

One of the things that set us up for our previous change in attitude about alcohol was the apparent failure of Prohibition. It would be a rare discussion of marijuana if the subject of Prohibition did not come up. During *that* ill-fated venture, we supposedly learned the futility of trying to legislate morality, particularly morality when it comes to this sort of issue—the use of chemical additives to make your head buzz—and so how are we not falling into the same trap again with this "war against drugs"?

I should mention in passing here the important point that keeping drugs illegal and conducting a "war on drugs" should not be considered the same thing. More about that later.

The first thing that needs to be said here is that what I write should not be taken as a brief for Prohibition. I *do* think Prohibition was a bad idea. But a couple of things should be said in defense of those who urged it, and were so motivated that they got the Constitution successfully amended—no easy feat—in pursuit of their goal. My ringing defense of them amounts to the mild observation that they were not *all* crazy wowsers.

Prohibition was basically a time when America went into detox. And the way we had been behaving prior to Prohibition would indicate that something very much like detox was badly needed. Bad things came out of Prohibition (like the establishment of the Mafia), but the time in detox did do us *some* good. Alcohol abuse prior to Prohibition was a glaring social problem, and the people who sought to address it with a complete ban on alcohol were not fighting with a bogeyman. Their solution was *not* a biblical one, as I hope to explain below, but the problem they were seeking to address was not imaginary. The fact that an amendment to the Constitution was passed over this issue would seem to indicate that alcohol abuse was understood to be at crisis levels.

So while Prohibition might have been understandable, why would I say that it was unbiblical? And if I believe that marijuana use should remain illegal, then what are the societal and biblical differences between marijuana use and alcohol use?

When unbelieving civil authorities legislate against the mere use of wine, for example, they are doing so contrary to the teaching of the Bible. If the magistrate prohibits the use of wine at a Sabbath dinner of believers, he is clearly overreaching. This does not mean that he must be disregarded—that civil disobedience is *necessarily* required—but it does mean that the magistrate has set himself against the clear teaching of the Bible.

That segment of the Christian church which happens to agree with this kind of prohibitionism is a very provincial portion of the church—American Christianity over the last century or so.

But when the magistrate outlaws the use of marijuana, he is not contradicting Scripture in the same way. Let me make this point particularly clear. I want to argue that marijuana use is clearly sinful, but I am not debating *at this point* whether it should be criminal. That is for a later chapter. For our purposes here, I am simply arguing that if the magistrate treats marijuana as something to be banned, this is not in the same category as Prohibition. This is because Scripture recognizes a number of lawful uses for alcohol, but does not do so for substances like pot.

So in states where marijuana use is still against the law, Christians who want to approve the use of it anyway do not occupy the same moral high ground that Christ would have occupied had the wedding at Cana taken place during Prohibition and been raided by ATF agents.

In arguing that marijuana use is sinful, it is important to note what is meant by "marijuana use." The proposition being argued here is that it is sinful to ingest marijuana to any extent that alters the chemistry of the body in order to cause a physiological response of any magnitude. I am not arguing that there is any sin inherent in the marijuana plant, and I am told that it can be used in the making of fine ropes. I am not saying that it would be a sin to hold marijuana in the hand, or to sprinkle it over the top of one's head. I am not saying that it would be a sin to ingest marijuana in minuscule amounts, amounts that have no effect whatever.

Such distinctions are necessary because the sinful mind is legalistic and always wants to push boundaries. People take dope for the *effect*, and I am going to be arguing that it is a sin to seek this particular effect. It is a sin to seek the stronger forms of it—getting loaded—and it is a sin to seek the milder forms of it—getting a pleasant, euphoric buzz. If marijuana has done its work *as a drug*, then that work has been a sinful one.

In what follows, the observations are made on the basis of objective knowledge of marijuana use, and not on the basis of self-reports from drug users who want to recommend the drug. We know a great deal about marijuana—it is a destroyer, as we will show later—and the hard data we have cannot be waved off as establishment hysteria over reefer madness.

Because marijuana is a toxic drug, getting to the point of physiological response happens rapidly. Unlike wine, for example, marijuana has an immediate effect, within minutes. Two sips of wine tastes good. Two hits from a joint, and the process of intoxication has begun.

The active ingredient in marijuana is THC, and over recent decades, THC potency has regularly increased. In the sixties, ordinary marijuana averaged one-half of 1 percent THC. Today the average is 3 percent, with some forms (sinsemilla) getting to an average of 7.5 percent. The half life of THC in the body is three to seven days.

Contrast this with the half life of alcohol, which is about an hour or two. Marijuana smokers frequently think that they do not have a problem with the drug because "they only smoke on weekends." But by the next weekend, half the THC is still in the body and is still having an effect.

Even after the high has worn off, THC continues to impair the body's ability to function. For a chronic user, it can take months before the THC is out of the system, and even then, permanent effects on the ability to think can be measured and observed. THC has an effect on the nerve cells in the brain where memories are formed. This is not a datum seen only in the laboratory. Those who are acquainted with drug users recognize at once the problem of "the space cadet." Marijuana users frequently lose their motivation to work (which is the last thing a young man needs), their concern over their appearance, and their grasp of ethical standards. Obviously, heavy users will be more heavily affected, but to the extent that they are affected at all, they are harmfully (and sinfully) affected.

Now that we have set the stage, what does the Bible teach?

> *Therefore let us not sleep, as do others; but let us watch and be sober. For they that sleep sleep in the night; and they that be drunken are drunken in the night. But let us, who are of the day, be sober, putting on the breastplate of faith and love; and for an helmet, the hope of salvation. (1 Thess. 5:6–8)*

The Greek word translated "sober" here is *nepho*, and it means to "be self-possessed under all circumstances." Being sober is utterly inconsistent with every form of mental and spiritual drunkenness. Someone who is affected to any extent by marijuana is not sober in the sense that Paul uses that word. Peter says the same thing, using the same word.

> *Wherefore gird up the loins of your mind, be sober, and hope to the end for the grace that is to be brought unto you at the revelation of Jesus Christ.* (1 Pet. 1:13)

It is very interesting that Peter couples this requirement to be sober with the requirement to "gird up the loins of your mind." This figure of speech is striking; girding up the loins is gathering up the robes, preparing for action. The Christian mind is to be in training, preparing to think clearly and with godly precision. A lack of sobriety, a lack of *nephos*, to any extent, is completely inconsistent with this. Two drags on a joint and nephos is impaired. The clear-mindedness that is required is necessary for prayer: "But the end of all things is at hand: be ye therefore sober, and watch unto prayer" (1 Pet. 4:7).

A related word is *nephalios,* and the mindset behind it is required of Christian elders as they set an example for the congregation. This word means to be "in control of one's thought processes," and to be "sober-minded, to be well-composed in mind."

> *A bishop then must be blameless, the husband of one wife, vigilant, sober, of good behaviour, given to hospitality, apt to teach. (1 Tim. 3:2)*

We know from the immediate context that the required sobriety is consistent with the drinking of wine in moderation. Paul says in the next verse that the elder is not to be given to wine. The use of wine in moderation is consistent with *nephos*. But nothing in what we know of marijuana makes it consistent with this biblical requirement.

To smoke marijuana in order to get any level of euphoria from it is clearly a sin. Reasoning by analogy, we can also see that drug use is a sin too because it is designed to bring about the one state—brain fog—which is condemned as a lawless application of alcohol or intoxication. "And do not be drunk with wine, in which is dissipation; but be filled with the Spirit" (Eph. 5:18, NKJV).

The objection is often made that this excludes getting drunk with wine and does not exclude getting a buzz from marijuana. This is a good illustration of the legalistic, hairsplitting mindset of those who are attached to their sin. We too often think that legalism, the drawing of unscriptural boundaries, is the province of the overly righteous. But legalism is a sinful frame of mind, and it does not disappear even in the midst of licentious behavior. Sinners love to catch at words—"it all depends on what *is* is"—and we need to realize what is going on when they do this.

When someone says that Paul prohibits "drunkenness" but not "getting high," we have an example of this kind of catching at words. Paul also says not to get drunk with *wine*. Does that mean that gin is all right? Beer? Rubbing alcohol?

If a man gets drunk with beer regularly, and the church disciplines him, may they use Ephesians 5:18 as part of their basis for doing so? The only reasonable answer is of course. Paul says not to get drunk with wine because it is one example of dissipation. Anyone who thinks that wine is the only route to dissipation doesn't get around much. The Greek word for "dissipation" here is *asotia*, referring to a life that is prodigal or dissolute.

The Greek word for "drunk" is *methusko*, which refers to intoxication. If a man smokes dope until he is facedown on the carpet, he is disobeying Ephesians 5:18. *How* he got loaded is not the point. If he got there with gin, beer, wine, or dope, the problem is the same. He is not sober-minded. As we have already seen, marijuana has an intoxicating effect almost immediately. This intoxicated state is unlawful, however induced.

TAKEAWAY #1: SMOKING MARIJUANA NECESSITATES INTOXICATION.

CHAPTER TWO

SOBRIETY AND DRUNKENNESS

As we consider the biblical teaching on marijuana use, we should want to take a close look at what the Scriptures teach about drunkenness. Although there is not a close parallel between alcohol and marijuana (as discussed in the previous chapter), there *is* a close analogy between being drunk and being stoned.

Any fair-minded reader of the Scriptures will come away with the impression that the Bible takes a dim view of being drunk. We will look at that teaching in close detail here, then look at some examples of drunkenness in the historical narrative, and then draw some applications to the question of marijuana use. At the end of the chapter we will look at some of the positive things that Scripture says about alcohol—and show how those descriptions do not apply to marijuana use.

Sins are like grapes; they come in bunches. In a number of the passages I cite here, please notice how drunkenness keeps sorry company. Sins tend to cluster, and when you go down into the middle of that crowd, you are more likely to find a pot dealer there than, say, if you were at a quilting bee.

Let's begin with an observation from the apostle Peter:

> *For the time past of our life may suffice us to have wrought the will of the Gentiles, when we walked in lasciviousness, lusts, excess of wine, revellings, banquetings, and abominable idolatries: wherein they think it strange that ye run not with them to the same excess of riot, speaking evil of you. (1 Pet. 4:3–4)*

What these people have in common is that they are all engaged in a hedonistic pursuit of sensual pleasure. They all want to get laid and loaded. The name of the game is sensory overload. Now if I were looking for a place to shelve "stoned out of his gourd," would I be more likely to put it after *joy* and before *peace*, or after *excess of wine* and before *revelling*?

And when a phrase like *excess of riot* is used, the apostle Peter is expecting us to be able to fill in the blanks. The Greek word rendered "riot" here is *asotia* (introduced in the last chapter), and it refers to a dissolute manner of life. A fellow has a dissolute manner of life, and he is running a surplus on it. The Scriptures don't have to spell out for us that the apostle is not referring to the world of stamp collectors, or bird photographers who specialize in hummingbirds. That phrase "excess of riot" could just as easily be talking about beer as gin, or meth as crack cocaine, or pot as vodka. We know what is being addressed here.

The company you keep matters.

Again, the apostle Paul says this: "And be not drunk with wine, wherein is excess; but be filled with the Spirit" (Eph. 5:18).

The command as given is to avoid drunkenness with wine, and Paul then describes the problem with it. It is *excess*. The word here is *asotia*, as above, which means "dissipation, debauchery, or other forms of loose living." Now who in their right mind would think that Paul is simply prohibiting drunkenness with *wine*? Does anybody think that Paul would be fine with *asotia*, provided the bender were fueled with margaritas?

God says *no* to excess because He has something better prepared for us, which is the filling of the Spirit. He says *no* to us for the same reason that a mother who has been preparing her son's favorite meal all afternoon will tell him *no* if he comes into the kitchen to get a bag of chips half an hour before dinnertime. She says *no*, not because she is a killjoy but because she *isn't*. She is concerned that he will ruin his appetite and not be able to enjoy something which she knows he will enjoy far more than the chips.

In the same way, we are not to get wrecked through excess because this will interfere with the Spirit's work in us.

We sometimes think of this passage telling us that the Spirit is the substance with which we are to be filled. I believe a better rendering of it would be that we are to be filled *by means of* the Spirit. In other words, the Spirit is not the "fluid" that fills us but rather the agent who is doing the pouring of that which fills us.

There is a parallel passage in Colossians that results in the same psalms, hymns, and spiritual songs, and this parallel passage gives us an indication of what the Spirit is supposed to fill us with:

> *Let the word of Christ dwell in you richly in all wisdom; teaching and admonishing one another in psalms and hymns and spiritual songs, singing with grace in your hearts to the Lord. (Col. 3:16)*

If we put these two passages together, we get something like this: "Let the word of Christ dwell in you richly, by means of the Holy Spirit, such that you teach and admonish one another...."

The Holy Spirit takes the Scriptures, *all of them*, and applies them to our lives. And when they are applied to our lives, we find that they have been applied to our drinking and smoking habits.

In Proverbs, we find that Scripture takes a dim view of this kind of excess in the Old Testament as well: "Wine is a mocker, strong drink is raging: and whosoever is deceived thereby is not wise" (Prov. 20:1).

This is said of wine and strong drink, which have *legitimate* uses as described elsewhere, and which I will explain below. How much more would it apply to a substance that *only* intoxicated the one who took it?

We are also warned against the deceitfulness of such things. When a man wants to loosen his grip on sobriety, he wants to be given excuses that enable him to feel good about doing so: "Look not thou upon the wine when it is red, when it giveth his colour in the cup, when it moveth itself aright" (Prov. 23:31).

In yet another reminder that sins are like grapes, we have this observation from the apostle Paul: "Let us walk honestly, as in the day; not in rioting and drunkenness, not in chambering and wantonness, not in strife and envying" (Rom. 13:13).

The meaning of "walk honestly" here is obvious. And if someone says that behavior at a rave only counts as "rioting" if the person concerned is running counterclockwise around the dance floor, then he is the person being the legalist and not the person concerned about his behavior. We don't need the apostle to add "or getting stoned" right after drunkenness to know that it is included.

A dissolute lifestyle is actively discouraged in Scripture.

> *It is not for kings, O Lemuel, it is not for kings to
> drink wine; nor for princes strong drink: lest they
> drink, and forget the law, and pervert the judg-
> ment of any of the afflicted. (Prov. 31:4–5)*

And if someone objects that this part of Proverbs is addressed to royalty, to kings, I grant the point. But I would want to push it in the opposite direction. This is not limited to kings, such that peasants may give way to drunkenness. No, the book of Proverbs is given to all God's people. And the word that means "to speak a proverb" is also a word that means "to rule." Learning to live in accordance with the proverbs God gave us is preparation for dominion. And living in a dissolute lifestyle is the way that many among the nobility have lost their position.

> *Now the works of the flesh are manifest, which are
> these; Adultery, fornication, uncleanness, lasciv-
> iousness, idolatry, witchcraft, hatred, variance,
> emulations, wrath, strife, seditions, heresies, en-
> vyings, murders, drunkenness, revellings, and
> such like: of the which I tell you before, as I have
> also told you in time past, that they which do such
> things shall not inherit the kingdom of God. (Gal.
> 5:19–21)*

But the fact that alcohol can be abused does not negate a right scriptural use for it. And it is in this aspect of it that we can see a wide divergence between a bottle of beer and a joint.

> *He causeth the grass to grow for the cattle, and*
> *herb for the service of man: that he may bring*
> *forth food out of the earth; and wine that maketh*
> *glad the heart of man, and oil to make his face to*
> *shine, and bread which strengtheneth man's heart.*
> *(Ps. 104:14–15)*

And lest anyone's heart leap for joy because it mentions herbs "for the service of man," it is talking about your *salad*, and not about your stash.

Now applying the principle that we have been following here, the text says that wine gladdens the heart of man, and there is no problem if we grant that beer and scotch can do exactly the same thing. Different means to the same end. But marijuana leads straight to the incapacitated end that is prohibited in all alcohol use.

The apostle Paul urges Timothy to take a little wine for medicinal purposes: "Drink no longer water, but use a little wine for thy stomach's sake and thine often infirmities" (1 Tim. 5:23).

We are also told that there is a legitimate celebratory use for wine: "Go thy way, eat thy bread with joy, and drink thy wine with a merry heart; for God now accepteth thy works" (Eccles. 9:7).

There is no inconsistency between drinking wine and holiness. In fact, drinking wine in the presence of the Lord is a manifestation of holiness.

> *The LORD hath sworn by his right hand, and by*
> *the arm of his strength, Surely I will no more give*
> *thy corn to be meat for thine enemies; and the sons*

> *of the stranger shall not drink thy wine, for the which thou hast laboured: but they that have gathered it shall eat it, and praise the LORD; and they that have brought it together shall drink it in the courts of my holiness. (Isaiah 62:8–9)*

Like all good gifts, it is possible for someone to use their liberty with wine in such a way that someone else is stumbled. And the New Testament warns us to be careful in this department.

> *But if thy brother be grieved with thy meat, now walkest thou not charitably. Destroy not him with thy meat, for whom Christ died. Let not then your good be evil spoken of: for the kingdom of God is not meat and drink; but righteousness, and peace, and joy in the Holy Ghost. For he that in these things serveth Christ is acceptable to God, and approved of men. Let us therefore follow after the things which make for peace, and things wherewith one may edify another. For meat destroy not the work of God. All things indeed are pure; but it is evil for that man who eateth with offence. It is good neither to eat flesh, nor to drink wine, nor any thing whereby thy brother stumbleth, or is offended, or is made weak. (Rom. 14:15–21)*

And of course, we may finish with the famous episode of the Lord's miracle at the wedding of Cana. If the use of wine was sinful and problematic, then it would have been really problematic for Jesus to have made 160 gallons of it.

And when they wanted wine, the mother of Jesus saith unto him, They have no wine. Jesus saith unto her, Woman, what have I to do with thee? mine hour is not yet come. His mother saith unto the servants, Whatsoever he saith unto you, do it. And there were set there six waterpots of stone, after the manner of the purifying of the Jews, containing two or three firkins apiece. Jesus saith unto them, Fill the waterpots with water. And they filled them up to the brim. And he saith unto them, Draw out now, and bear unto the governor of the feast. And they bare it. When the ruler of the feast had tasted the water that was made wine, and knew not whence it was: (but the servants which drew the water knew;) the governor of the feast called the bridegroom, and saith unto him, Every man at the beginning doth set forth good wine; and when men have well drunk, then that which is worse: but thou hast kept the good wine until now. This beginning of miracles did Jesus in Cana of Galilee, and manifested forth his glory; and his disciples believed on him. (John 2:3–11)

TAKEAWAY #2: BEING DRUNK AND BEING STONED ARE INCONSISTENT WITH CHRISTIAN HOLINESS. NEVERTHELESS, ALCOHOL CONSUMPTION IS NOT INCONSISTENT WITH HOLINESS.

CHAPTER THREE

MORE SUPERFICIAL COMPARISONS

Suppose all this is granted, but a further question is asked. What about the fellow who is not wiped out? He smokes marijuana but remains (at least in his own mind) fully functional. He grants that "drunkenness" is always wrong but denies that marijuana has to produce "drunkenness." Why cannot cannabis provide an equivalent experience to wine gladdening the heart of man (Ps. 104:15)?

We have to look at this argument carefully. We have seen that drunkenness is flatly prohibited by Scripture, but we have to recognize that other uses of alcohol are approved and encouraged throughout the Bible.

In order to do this, we must back up. According to the Bible, alcohol has at least five lawful scriptural uses. Let's look at each and see if there is a parallel to marijuana at that point. The last one we will consider is the "gladden the heart" argument.

The first use of alcohol is sacramental.

> *And he took the cup, and gave thanks, and gave it to them, saying, Drink ye all of it; For this is my blood of the new testament, which is shed for many for the remission of sins. But I say unto you, I will not drink henceforth of this fruit of the vine, until that day when I drink it new with you in my Father's kingdom. (Matt. 26:27–29)*

From Genesis to Revelation, we have no scriptural warrant for the use of drugs in worship. While this is a feature of numerous unbelieving sects and cults, it has no part of biblical worship. God does require wine in the Lord's Supper, but He does not require any use of marijuana sacramentally.

Wine also has medicinal value. "Drink no longer water, but use a little wine for thy stomach's sake and thine often infirmities" (1 Tim. 5:23). Here we have to say that marijuana *could* be scripturally lawful if it were being used in a genuinely medicinal way. With this said, at the same time, we have to say that the current political push to allow for the medicinal use of marijuana does have a hidden agenda behind it—the issue is not medicine, but rather the legalization and normalization of marijuana use. The current science indicates that the proposed medical value of marijuana is being greatly overrated. It is being pushed as a medicine for non-medicinal reasons.

Third, there is the aesthetic dimension.

> *Every man at the beginning doth set forth good wine; and when men have well drunk, then that which is worse: but thou hast kept the good wine until now. (John 2:10)*

One wine might be selected because it would go well with the beef, and another chosen because it complemented the pasta.

Marijuana goes well with (recalling Cheech and Chong) Oreos and mustard. We have no scriptural reference to drug use as an aesthetic gift, but we do have a scriptural acknowledgment of aesthetic standards with wine: "No man also having drunk old wine straightway desireth new: for he saith, The old is better" (Luke 5:39).

We also drink in order to quench our thirst.

> *After this, Jesus knowing that all things were now accomplished, that the scripture might be fulfilled, saith, I thirst. Now there was set a vessel full of vinegar: and they filled a sponge with vinegar [cheap wine], and put it upon hyssop, and put it to his mouth. When Jesus therefore had received the vinegar, he said, It is finished: and he bowed his head, and gave up the ghost. (John 19:28–30)*

We see here that wine satisfies a God-given desire, that of thirst. We have no scriptural reason to think that marijuana satisfies any such natural desire. On the contrary, marijuana creates a number of additional desires.

And last, wine has a wonderful celebratory function.

> *He causeth the grass to grow for the cattle, and herb for the service of man: that he may bring forth food out of the earth; and wine that maketh glad the heart of man, and oil to make his face to shine, and bread which strengtheneth man's heart.*
> *(Ps. 104:14–15)*

When a Thanksgiving table is set, when the rolls are brown and buttered, when the turkey is done, and the crystal glasses are filled with wonderful wines, there the hearts of believers are filled with gladness. But when a room is filled with sweet, sticky smoke, the hearts of those present are filled with nothing but self-deception. True celebration is a *discipline*, accompanied with hard work, planning, training, and the fruition of joy. The use of marijuana is a celebratory slide downward, indulged in by the lazy and self-indulgent.

But doesn't this passage say that God also gives herbs "for the service of man?" Yes, but drugs are not at all in view. The Hebrew word is *eseb* and refers to herbs, green plants, and grass. It is talking about plants that work on behalf of man, not plants that cause a man's mind to become blurry. The lesson here is to eat your vegetables and salads.

Of all these, the only possible lawful use for marijuana is the medicinal, and the use to which everyone puts marijuana is the one that is denied to alcohol. In short, if someone was affected by alcohol the way they are affected within minutes of taking just a few hits of marijuana, I would insist they have had too much to drink. Why? Because their mind has been noticeably blunted; they are no longer sober-minded; they have started visibly down the road of dissipation.

This is admittedly a judgment call. In just a few pages, we will be consider the biblical necessity of such judgment calls.

One word in the New Testament related to drug use is *pharmakeia*. It is the word in Galatians 5:20 rendered as "sorcery" or "witchcraft." In the first century, the use of "altered state of consciousness" drugs was clearly connected in various ways to the occult. In the ancient usage, *pharmakeia* is usually used to describe some occult practice related to drug use—potions, drugs, and so forth. This means that the translation of "sorcery" in Galatians 5:20 is probably a good one. But even today, the connection between drug use and occult practices is not entirely severed.

Even when there is no occultism, this does not make the prohibition of *pharmakeia* irrelevant to the modern "secular" drug user. Ancient drug use was far more "religious" than modern drug use. But so was ancient prostitution. So when Paul commands the Corinthians to stay away from prostitutes, contextually the problem he was attacking was prostitution mixed with idolatry. In other words, men who worshiped at the Temple of Aphrodite would do so by having sex with the prostitutes there. This mixture of sin categories does not keep us from seeing the pastoral relevance of 1 Corinthians 6:12–20 to a modern "secular" use of prostitutes. In other words, a modern man could not defend his night with a hooker by maintaining that she was not a priestess.

In the same way, *pharmakeia* encompasses more than one sin. One of them is the use of drugs. We may also reason in the other direction. If we were to describe modern pot smoking to an ancient Greek speaker, and we asked him what word would be used to describe this practice (with no occultism in sight), he would still answer *pharmakeia:* the first definition of this word in *Thayer's Greek English lexcion* is "the use or the administering of drugs." The second definition is "poisoning," and the third "witchcraft." *Liddell and Scott's Greek English Lexicon* says much the same. First, it is the use of "drugs, potions, spells." The second definition is "poisoning or witchcraft." *Vine's Complete Expository Dictionary* says the word "primarily signified the use of medicine, drugs, spells; then, poisoning; then, sorcery."

With these things in mind, the warning that Paul gives after he has listed the works of the flesh should be sobering to those who want to smoke dope as part of their Christian liberty. He says that "they which do such things shall not inherit the kingdom of God" (Gal. 6:21). An awful lot rides on this.

Discussions over marijuana frequently find themselves diverted into interesting but irrelevant side paths. One of the characteristics of sophomoric insight is the ability to make superficial connections where no genuine comparison exists. The purpose of this short section is simply to show why it isn't a longer one.

The first superficial comparison has already been addressed—the moderate drinking of wine, or other forms of alcohol, cannot be compared to the immediate intoxicating effects of marijuana. At the same time, it must be said that with some very potent forms of alcohol, the possibility of comparison does exist. Rubbing alcohol would be ingested only for the sake of immediate effect, and so a comparison could be made. But in the vast majority of cases, the two activities are not comparable.

Another superficial comparison can be made to the smoking of tobacco. But tobacco is a room-smell-altering substance, but it is not a mind-altering substance. There are a number of very good reasons not to smoke cigarettes, but for the most part they are not the same reasons for avoiding marijuana.

However, because tobacco is on the fast track to being declared "a drug" by our federal masters, it is important for us to think biblically here as well. Some pietists have maintained that all tobacco use is necessarily sinful. A mindless response to this is that no tobacco use is sinful. But this is clearly false. Tobacco use can be sinful for various reasons, even though it is not automatically sinful. If a man smokes a pipe once a month, I would be hard-pressed to show from the Bible how he was sinning.

But if he is addicted to a pack of Camels a day, and cannot go without them apart from getting the shakes, then obvious issues of self-control come to mind. And the same thing goes for someone's favorite Starbucks mocha.

Marijuana is a mind-altering drug; it affects perception and one's ability to think. With "drugs" like coffee and tobacco, and anything else like that we might think of, the issue is not the loss of reason, because these are not mind-altering agents. But they do affect the body, and so the issue can be the creation of bodily dependencies, and a consequent loss of joy. The body is hard enough to subdue (Rom. 6:12) without giving it a bunch of extra dependencies.

> *All things are lawful for me, but all things are not helpful. All things are lawful for me, but I will not be brought under the power of any. Foods for the stomach and the stomach for foods, but God will destroy both it and them. (1 Cor. 6:12–13, NKJV)*

"I will not be brought," Paul says, "under the power of any."

So the use of tobacco can easily be a moral issue. It just isn't this moral issue.

TAKEAWAY #3: ALCOHOL BENEFITS US IN FIVE WAYS, ACCORDING TO SCRIPTURE. MARIJUANA CANNOT FUNCTION IN THESE SAME WAYS.

CHAPTER FOUR

THE MEANING OF LIBERTY

In order to speak intelligently about the rights and wrongs of marijuana use, we must early on establish what kind of world we are discussing the question in. And the question that is hovering in the background of all such discussion is this: What is the meaning of liberty? In order to make any progress at all when it comes to understanding the use of marijuana, we have to know what freedom is. We also have to discuss it, and work through it carefully, with very sober minds. That means we should debate the question of pot without having smoked any.

In our secular and very individualistic time, liberty is frequently defined *simply as* the absence of coercion. And on one level, this is quite correct. If you are not chained to a dungeon wall, then you are obviously at liberty. This is true as far as it goes, which isn't very far if you're chained to the wall.

The problems begin when we treat this as the only definition of liberty. But there are layers. There are other issues involved in this. If I were to drive just a few miles to my west, into Washington State, I would there be at liberty to smoke marijuana. But because I would still be a Christian after that short drive, I would not be at liberty at all to smoke marijuana. Now because both of these statements are true, I would be at liberty and I would not be at liberty to perform a particular action. This means that being at liberty has more than one sense. The action might be legal and not moral.

> *Being then made free from sin, ye became the servants of righteousness. I speak after the manner of men because of the infirmity of your flesh: for as ye have yielded your members servants to uncleanness and to iniquity unto iniquity; even so now yield your members servants to righteousness unto holiness. For when ye were the servants of sin, ye were free from righteousness. What fruit had ye then in those things whereof ye are now ashamed? for the end of those things is death. But now being made free from sin, and become servants to God,*

> *ye have your fruit unto holiness, and the end ev-*
> *erlasting life. For the wages of sin is death; but the*
> *gift of God is eternal life through Jesus Christ our*
> *Lord. (Rom. 6:18–23)*

The Greek word rendered as "servants" here is *doulos*, or "slave." We have slaves of unrighteousness described here, and we have slaves of righteousness described. The slaves of righteousness are characterized by their freedom, and the slaves of unrighteousness are characterized by their bondage. Slaves of righteousness are free from unrighteousness, which is to say, they are free from the real bondage. But this point should not be missed—they are free from bondage because they are a different kind of slave.

The reason I would not be at liberty to smoke dope in Washington State is because I am a *slave*. I am a slave to Christ, which means I can't do certain things. One of things I am prohibited from doing is using my liberty as a device for enslaving myself. These are liberty chains—you may not use your liberty (which is real) as a cover for tying yourself up in bondage again.

Christian liberty is freedom *to* do the will of God, but the flip side of this is equally clear. It is freedom *from* practices that enslave: "For, brethren, ye have been called unto liberty; only use not liberty for an occasion to the flesh, but by love serve one another" (Gal. 5:13).

In other words, if a Christian has been called to liberty, is he free to smoke pot? Well, is getting buzzed an "occasion to the flesh"? Since the obvious and clear answer is "Yes, it is an occasion to the flesh," then this means he is directly told not to use his liberty in that way.

This is how we maintain our liberty. This is how we stand fast in it: "Stand fast therefore in the liberty wherewith Christ hath made us free, and be not entangled again with the yoke of bondage" (Gal. 5:1).

Using our liberty for the purposes assigned to it is the way we avoid being entangled again. We serve Christ now, and no man can serve two masters.

In 1 Corinthians, the apostle is very clear that those who live wasted and dissolute lives are not going to inherit the kingdom (6:9–10). This sets the context for his comment that follows, when he says "all things are lawful" (v. 12). It would be false and ungodly to take the antinomian route and claim that because we are now under grace, we get to do absolutely anything we want. No, those who think *that* way are going to Hell.

> *All things are lawful unto me, but all things are not expedient: all things are lawful for me, but I will not be brought under the power of any. (1 Cor. 6:12)*

So what is Paul talking about when he says that "all things are lawful"? Contextually he is talking about things that are inexpedient, or things that exercise power over someone. The application I would suggest here is that of practices or substances that may be lawful in themselves but are potentially addicting, or practices or substances that are certainly addictive. The former could range from a coffee junkie to someone addicted to tobacco. These things are not sinful in themselves because they are not mind-altering and because they have innocent uses. But if someone is so dependent on coffee that they can't be a Christian in the morning until they have had some, then there is a problem.

When Paul says that he "will not be brought under the power of any," he appears to be saying that the human body already has a bunch of needs and wants that are yelling at us all the time. Some of them Paul is talking about in the immediate context. "Food for the stomach, and the stomach for food" (v. 13, NIV). Our bodies want sleep, air, sunshine, sex, water, meat, and so on. These desires are God-given, but because the world has been knocked cock-eyed by sin, they can become inordinate.

Now, who among us was doing so well with all these bodily demands, the ones that came with the hardware already installed, that we thought to upload a few more dependencies just to show how good we are at the self-discipline? Oh, you know, Smith was doing so well with hunger, thirst, and lust that he decided to add nicotine and alcohol.

Paul urges extreme caution. "I will not be brought under the power of any."

The latter would be things that are sinful to ingest in themselves (because they are mind-altering), but they also violate the principle set out in this passage. Crack cocaine is sinful in two ways—it violates the requirement that God has for us to be sober-minded, but it also brings the body (one that was already struggling) under the power of an additional substance. What sinner needs that?

So let us return to the stark alternatives set out in Romans 6. There are two directions we can take this, and one of them is (in my view) disastrous. Slavery to righteousness is something that can only be accomplished by the Holy Spirit of God. Freedom to do right is a true freedom, but it cannot be imposed on a citizenry by the civil magistrate. Congress is not able to pass a law that will make everyone virtuous.

At the same time, when this true Spirit-given freedom takes root in a citizenry, and the people are generally moral and religious, then (and only then) will it be possible to make room for any number of other forms of civic liberty.

On the other hand, when the people are dissolute, this means they are slaves to their sins. And one of the things that despots found out a long time ago is that slaves to sin have handles that can be used by rulers.

This is why John Adams once said that the American Constitution presupposed a moral and religious people. He went on to add that it was "wholly inadequate" for any other.

TAKEAWAY #4: LIBERTY TO SMOKE DOPE IS LIBERTY TO BE ENSLAVED.

CHAPTER FIVE

SINS AND CRIMES

Those who take the Bible seriously should be able to see right away that not all sins should be crimes. But we should also be able to see plainly that many "non-crimes" are clearly sinful. For example, covetousness is clearly a sin, a violation of the tenth commandment. God says not to covet anything that belongs to our neighbor, but the magistrate is not competent to deal with covetousness.

So I am not arguing here one way or the other with regard to the criminalization of marijuana use. We can at least say the magistrate should punish the criminal behavior that frequently accompanies such drug use, and the debate over whether the use of marijuana in itself should be against civil law can be left for another time. But even if the civil government legalized it, which it might, sanctions should still remain. Because it is so clearly wrong, the two other governments established by God should provide sanctions for any such drug use. The family and the church can (and should) discipline noncriminal sinful behavior.

We are living in a time when the cultural pressure to fold on various issues related to self-control is very intense. Because of this pressure, many Christians who know that smoking dope is obviously a sin are tempted to acquiesce to the pressure by giving way in places that do not seem to be quite as much of a compromise. In other words, why can't Christians give way to the pressure by allowing that while getting stoned may be *sin*, it ought not be a *crime*? Thus there appears to be a way out—we can surrender to the pressure to legalize pot while not seeming to ourselves like we are acting the role of political cowards.

Now, there is a principled libertarian position that could be argued (and that we will deal with as this chapter unfolds), but the *first* thing we have to deal with is that for many Christians, on many of these issues, the libertarian option is simply a safe harbor, a cop-out, a way of running away. We see this happening on homosexual marriage: "Why should the civil government be in the marriage business anyway?" And we see it in the downgrade of public morals on issues like gambling, pornography, and the use of drugs. We mutter to ourselves that it turns out that the Scriptures never prohibited all those things that unregenerate men are now clamoring that they be allowed to do.

But because many people assume that morality is *defined* by legality, it will be a short step for them to assume that once something is legal in all fifty states, we ought thereafter to celebrate that activity as one of the cardinal virtues.

Remember how rapidly we progressed from homosexuality simply being decriminalized to the point now where its celebration is *mandated* in virtually every public space. But morality is defined by Scripture and not by our legal codes. In the history of the world, all sorts of ungodliness has been legal, for pity's sake. I once saw a cartoon of a couple of explorers in a cannibal's pot, with the cannibals dancing around it. One of the explorers was saying to the other one, "You know, the way their laws are structured, this is all perfectly legal."

If we had a society in which hardly anyone got high, but someone ventured to suggest that we ought not to have a law against it, and they argued this on libertarian principles, it should be possible to have a debate about *only* that. But we are having *this* debate now because a large part of our population believes that this is an essential part of what constitutes the good life. They do not wish to be left alone to enjoy their private vice. They want our whole society to enter into their sticky-smoke nirvana.

How long will it be, once marijuana is legal everywhere, before any kind of marked disapproval of it is illegal everywhere? How long before employers are no longer allowed to "discriminate" on the basis of pot use? And while we are here, allow me to comment on what a great deal of use the devil has gotten from that infernal word *discriminate*.

Thus, because of the complexity of our society, it is not really possible to debate something like the legalization of marijuana as a stand-alone issue. One law might just be a little block of wood, but if it is located at the bottom of a swaying Jenga tower on your coffee table, then simply removing it might be harder than it initially appeared.

Marijuana laws are related to, and tangled up together with, employment law, welfare benefits, custody issues, traffic regulations, mental health issues, and public safety.

If a libertarian says that he believes smoking dope should be legal, and he says this on the basis of his convictions about personal liberty, then this reality provides us with a good way of testing whether he is a libertarian with sincere convictions across the board, or if he is simply someone who wants to smoke pot no matter what. On the basis of a libertarian set of convictions, we should not want the use of marijuana to be legal unless it is also equally legal for business owners to fire employees on the simple basis of marijuana use—and not just operators of heavy equipment either. In other words, the liberty to smoke pot and the liberty to fire a pothead should be the same liberty.

Otherwise, we are granting liberty to the privileges and no liberty at all to the responsibilities. That would mean that the civil magistrate is not playing the role of an impartial referee—rather, he would be actively advancing and promoting (and subsidizing) the use of marijuana. And to be honest, apart from such subsidies, the legalization of pot would probably not be *that* big a deal.

This is because a society that has truly embraced liberty will not be providing any kind of welfare payments to anyone, much less to drug addicts. Imagine, if you will, a world where no one with THC in his blood system was eligible for food stamps, and where no employer could suffer legal repercussions if he dismissed someone for pot use. The *market* would discipline a great deal of self-destructive behavior.

Put another way, under economic libertarianism, responsible citizens would be just as free as the irresponsible ones. The *way* the push for legal pot is happening now, the pressure is on us to increase the liberty of the irresponsible citizens while simultaneously decreasing the liberty of the responsible ones. That fact all by itself should reveal the play that is being run on us.

Let me reinforce, one more time, the argument that I am making in this chapter. The fact that something is a vice or bad habit does not mean that it should automatically be treated as a crime. What Christian would deny that covetousness is a sin? It is the tenth of the ten commandments, meaning that God considers it to be a most serious offense (Exod. 20:17). In the New Testament, the apostle Paul teaches us that covetousness is tantamount to idolatry (Eph. 5:5). And yet who in their right mind would want the magistrate to be authorized to form a federal agency called the Covetousness Cops, authorized to monitor whether or not a man had spent too much time in an automobile showroom, or if his wife had lingered too long over a Talbots catalog? The civil magistrate is not competent to weigh such heart matters, and only a madman would want them to.

And so we have a spectrum. On one end, pretty much everyone would agree that murder ought to be treated as a crime. And on the other end, pretty much everyone would agree that envying your older sister should not be, even though envy is one of the seven deadly sins.

The discussion about marijuana is a discussion about how public vices should be defined and, once we have defined them, what we should do about it.

If a man goes home after work and has one beer more than he should have (as far as God is concerned), but then goes to bed, should that be against the law? This, compared with the obvious problem of someone who is out in public after too many beers and is drunk and disorderly or is weaving down the highway.

When it comes to public safety, the magistrate and the population supporting the magistrate need to do a cost-benefit analysis. There are some vices that are simply private vices. Other vices are a direct threat to the general population. In one scenario, when a man has had slightly too much to drink, he wakes up in the morning with a slight headache. But if another man finishes off the evening at the tavern with one bourbon, one scotch, and one beer and then gets behind the wheel to drive his serpentine way home, he is a public hazard.

Moreover, he is a public hazard even if in this condition he has successfully driven home a hundred times before without killing anybody. He is a threat *every* time he gets behind the wheel like that. Does a society have the right to protect itself from this kind of behavior? The answer that most of us would give is *yes*.

Now there is a legitimate debate about whether society should fight this in an anticipatory way (pulling random motorists over and giving Breathalyzer tests) or in the way of retribution (punishing drunk drivers severely if they hurt or kill someone). These are the ways of prevention and deterrence, respectively. I prefer deterrence, but that is beside the point. The point is that individual behavior is something that society *can* take a collective interest in without that interest becoming tyrannical.

Allow me to use a ludicrous example, but I use it merely to illustrate the point. If the state required every citizen to do twenty sit-ups and twenty jumping jacks every morning because "society can take a collective interest in health," this would be tyrannical. But suppose, at the other end of the spectrum, the state outlawed a drug that caused a murderous psychotic episode in twenty-five percent of all who took it. This would mean that when a person is about to take it, the intervening cop doesn't know if this person is one of the seventy-five percent or one of the twenty-five percent. Is it tyranny if the cop doesn't wait to find out?

Under these circumstances, it would be odd if someone were to argue—for the sake of libertarian purity—that we have to wait until after the murderous episode before we take matters into our own hands. Is it really tyranny to try to prevent an all-but-inevitable tragedy? Why should society be forced to play Russian roulette this way? In other words, after we have distinguished sins from crimes, that is all well and good. But we also have to distinguish sins from almost inevitable crimes.

These are extreme examples so that we might fix the *principle* in our minds. Marijuana use is somewhere in the middle, as we will see in later chapters.

Let me give a metaphor from C.S. Lewis, and then modify it slightly.

> *There are two ways in which [humans go] wrong. One is when human individuals drift apart from one another, or else collide with one another and do one another damage, by cheating or bullying. The other is when things go wrong inside the individual—when the different parts of him (his different faculties and desires and so on) either drift apart or interfere with one another. You can get the idea plain if you think of us as a fleet of ships sailing in formation. The voyage will be a success only, in the first place, if the ships do not collide*

and get in one another's way; and, secondly, if each ship is seaworthy and has her engines in good order. As a matter of fact, you cannot have either of these two things without the other. If the ships keep on having collisions they will not remain seaworthy very long.[3]

Lewis compares humanity to a fleet of ships. Let me compare us to one ship. A man cannot say that because he blew a hole in the hull of the ship but did so entirely within the confines of his own stateroom, it cannot be the business of anyone else on board. And it might not be, so long as he keeps his stateroom door completely closed. But suppose further a number of the passengers start doing that. There comes a time when this fad of private stateroom explosions *becomes* the business of everyone.

At some point what people are doing in the privacy of their own staterooms becomes a matter of public concern.

TAKEAWAY #5: "FREEDOM" TO SMOKE POT MUST COME WITH THE "FREEDOM" TO FIRE A POTHEAD.

3. C. S. Lewis, *Mere Christianity* (New York: HarperOne, 2001), 71.

CHAPTER SIX

THE WRONG END

Another reason why the decriminalization of marijuana use is such a bad idea is because of the current cultural-political climate. And what I mean is this.

In the abstract, let us imagine an anarcho-libertarian paradise. I don't believe such a thing would actually *be* all that much of a paradise, but it would be better than now at least (although that, too, is a discussion for another time). For the sake of argument, let's just assume this paradise.

In that society, those who pursued lives of virtue and those who pursued lives of vice would be equally free. Now suppose further that we are trying to figure out how to get from where we currently are to that place in time.

In the current set-up, we have potheads and we have the people who try to employ them. We have potheads and we have the people behind the counter who determine whether or not they qualify for food stamps. We have potheads and we have people who live virtuous, productive, and sober lives. And in the current set-up, both kinds of people are hassled and provoked in various ways by the political establishment. The potheads can be arrested and fined for possession, and the small business owner can be drastically fined thousands of dollars for starting a successful business and employing eight or nine people. The fact that we call these fines *taxes* doesn't alter their economic impact, or the disincentives that come along with them.

Now in this climate, if you legalize pot *first*, you are keeping all the restrictions on the virtuous and you are liberating those in the grip of a particular vice. What this is going to mean is that in effect you will be subsidizing vice and penalizing virtue. Or, to be more precise, you are forcing virtue to subsidize vice. And because you always get more of what you subsidize and less of what you penalize, the end result is going to be destructive.

In other words, a man who works out in the field with oil drilling equipment can purchase marijuana legally and can get as loaded as he wants on the weekend. At the same time, the employer still has to abide by all the restrictions and processes that govern employment law. He can't simply find out that his employee got stoned a couple days before, and just give him a pink slip as a consequence. To repeat the point of the last chapter, in a completely free country, the guy could get stoned legally, but he could also be promptly and legally sacked for getting stoned legally.

Here's another example: in this nation with libertarian laws, there would be no restrictions on pot use, and so have at it. But there would also be no welfare payments, no food stamps, no subsidized housing, no union laws, and so on. This means there would be no safety net to speak of, or at least no publicly-funded safety net. This would be a problem because, as John Wayne once supposedly said, "Life is hard. It's harder if you're stupid."

Private charity would certainly be present and available, but private mercy ministry tends to place conditions and terms on the offered help. In other words, private charity would like the help to be genuine help out of the world of vice, instead of a subsidy for continuing to live in that world of vice.

And what this would mean is that drug abuse would cease being attractive as a form of recreation to middle class and lower middle class individuals who would not be able to pay for all the consequences themselves. Take away the safety net, and it is likely that the number of people experimenting with the trapeze bar will decrease significantly. But if you strengthen the safety net, making it cushier and bouncier, you might find yourself needing to install additional trapeze bars.

To bring our discussion back to marijuana use, to legalize pot use in a highly regulated economy is the same thing as requiring employers to pay for some of the pot. Suppose that everybody ought to be free to do virtually anything. Even then, to begin the process with debilitating activities that sap the energy of a culture and a people and to get to freeing up the industrious workers later is going to be a policy that has consequences that will be absolutely crammed with unintended consequences.

As mentioned earlier, John Adams once said that our Constitution presupposes a moral and a religious people, and was "wholly inadequate [for] any other." When a constitution was drafted for a free and virtuous people, and we try to make it work for a dissolute and wasted people, this will have the effect of declaring war on the few remaining citizens who want to live in a virtuous way.

This is an inescapable reality. It is not whether but which. It is not whether a nation will discipline a sector of its population, but rather which sector of the population it will discipline. For example, in California, in the aftermath of Proposition 47, a number of former felonies have been downgraded to misdemeanors, including theft. So if a thief makes sure to steal less than $950 worth of goods, that theft will remain a misdemeanor. Not only that, but he can do this *on a daily basis*, and it will never rise to the level of a felony. He can do it every day for a month, and be approaching 30K in stolen goods, and somehow not be approaching the status of a felon.

Now $949 can buy an adequate amount of pot, and this means that shop-owners are being forced to pay for the habits of shoplifters. And, if not shop-owners, whoever it is that is supplying the 30K. When it comes to crimes, the civil magistrate has to take sides. And if he does not take sides against the lawless and indigent, then by that choice, he is taking sides against the industrious.

In a statist economy, as ours is rapidly becoming, lifting restrictions on vice is *not* a sign of approaching liberty. Instead, it is a sign that tyrants would rather govern a populace that is addicted to chemicals than a people in love with liberty.

TAKEAWAY #6: LIFTING MARIJUANA RESTRICTIONS IN OUR STATIST ECONOMY IS JUST A WAY TO MAKE THE NON-SMOKERS PAY FOR IT.

CHAPTER SEVEN

MENTAL HEALTH AND RISK

We have to begin this chapter by anticipating and acknowledging a number of different possible objections to what I am going to be arguing. My argument is that marijuana use is a significant factor in either causing or exacerbating violent psychotic episodes in regular users.

I want to begin with the anticipated objections because the concerns I am about to raise are far too easily and readily dismissed. Whether or not it is *fair* that they are so easily dismissed is rather beside the point. I want to argue that they are dismissed so handily because we have been conditioned or trained to dismiss them in this way, but for all that, we still have to answer the objections.

Some of my argumentation will be statistical, and so let me begin by saying that I fully understand that correlation does not necessarily mean causation. Coupled with this is the fact that mental health is not a straightforward and simple thing, like putting the eight ball in the corner pocket. With a billiard ball, the one causal factor would appear to be the cue, unless somebody is cheating. With someone's mental health, we could be talking about genetics, upbringing, medical history, drug use, early childhood trauma, and so on.

But when dealing with large populations and large sample sizes, at some point correlations should arouse suspicions. At some point someone should start to generate a hypothesis that can be pursued with further testing.

And when we consider such correlations, we should make sure we are using equal weights and measures in our arguments. We all know there is a correlation between smoking cigarettes and lung cancer. Furthermore, we don't require a 100 percent correlation before we say that cigarettes "cause cancer." But if we are talking about males, and the rate of lung cancer among heavy smokers, about one in four will get lung cancer. That means that three out of four heavy smokers will go to their graves not having made the surgeon general's point for him. Now, using *those* weights and measures, what correlations might we want to consider when it comes to heavy marijuana use?

A large part of our problem is that we live in a generation that has politicized pretty much everything. This means that certain hypotheses, *whatever* the levels of correlation, are simply off limits. They may be off limits for racial reasons, or gender equity reasons, or sunk-costs reasons. So depending on the circumstances, to seriously propose that something even be *researched* is to put your job and/or reputation in jeopardy. What do I mean?

Our society does not *want* certain things to be questioned. For example, if someone were to say that we ought to check into whether there is a link between autism and vaccinations, there would be (and has been) widespread support for the idea. But if someone suggested that we should check into the rise of autism and a broader use of daycare centers, the general response would be a white sheet of fury. The same kind of thing goes for birth control pills and ovarian cancer. Because of the anticipated level of demand for them, certain practices (and products) are *coddled*. They are not subjected to the same kind of review that other products are subjected to. This is because there is money to be made there.

Lest anyone panic, my point here is *not* that daycare centers cause autism, or that birth control pills cause cancer. The point is that in our political climate such notions will not even be allowed as *hypotheses*. In other words, on certain issues, social politics dictate to us what the possible problems might be, and which practices and products are not candidates for any kind of restrictions.

But medical science is supposed to be about the pursuit of *truth*, not the pursuit of tolerable truths.

I use these examples as a lead-in to the actual problem under discussion: Is marijuana use a contributing factor in some episodes of violent psychosis? The answer would appear to be that this is quite a reasonable hypothesis, and that it should be researched thoroughly. Not only should it be researched thoroughly, but it should be researched thoroughly without any vested interests demanding that the researchers discover only acceptable results.

Allow me to test your reactions to this:

> *The first four states that legalized marijuana for recreational use—Alaska, Colorado, Oregon, and Washington—have seen their rates of murder and aggravated assault increase much faster than the United States' rates as a whole since legalization. The gap has increased every year.[4]*

> *[Uruguay] began retail sales in the fall of 2017; in the first six months of 2018, murders in Uruguay rose 64 percent compared to the same period in 2017. Coincidence, no doubt.[5]*

If your reaction is "That can't be true" or if it is "I knew it all along!", then you are simply continuing whatever political game you have been playing, with marijuana use simply serving as the current football. If your reaction is "Perhaps this issue needs more careful

4. Alex Berenson, *Tell Your Children: The Truth about Marijuana, Mental Illness and Violence* (New York: Free Press, 2019), 180.
5. *Tell Your Children*, 222.

study," and "Perhaps we shouldn't revamp our marijuana laws until we know more about it," then you are being the adult in the room.

This really is a reasonable question. Moreover, it is a reasonable question where we have every right to believe the answer is obtainable. But we don't want to listen to reasonable questions because, as a culture, we already know what we want to do.

> *There is probably no other issue on which journalists rely so heavily on the lobby of a special interest, and pay so little attention to scientists, policy experts and specialists in the field.[6]*

But it remains a reasonable question. So why is it a reasonable question?

Just as individuals do, societies have the right to self-defense. When someone deliberately attacks someone else, the victim has the right to fight off the assailant. But this right to self-defense does not include the right to demand that everyone else behave in such a way as to present absolutely zero risk to others. God governs the world in such a way that risk cannot be brought down to zero, and it would be sinful to attempt it.

For example, if you get behind the wheel of a car and take to the highway, this means that all the other motorists who are driving the same stretch of road are presenting you with a lethal risk. This is a tolerable risk, and you are presenting a similar risk to them. Let's say

6. Ed Gogek, *Marijuana Debunked* (Asheville, NC: innerQuest: 2015), kindle location 244.

that their choice to drive is presenting you with a 1 in 100,000 chance of dying today. Something could go wrong, and sometimes it does. They might not stay on their side of the road. You might not stay on yours.

But the fact that this is the case, and we are all good with it, does not mean that someone has the right to play Russian roulette with you. He puts one bullet in a six-chambered gun, spins the chamber, walks up behind you, and pulls the trigger. A one in six chance is an intolerable risk, with the additional factor of *his* entertainment being a miserable benefit in the trade-off for that risk.

And if all the chambers were loaded, that would make things even worse. If the chances are six out of six that the victim will die, then that is not "chance" or "high risk," but rather murder.

So we have both intolerable risk and tolerable risk. But it is a mistake to speak simply of tolerable risk— we also need to speak of those levels where the desire to *avoid* risk is intolerable. I was once talking with a farmer friend, and somebody mentioned how early he had gotten up. His response was pertinent, and vigorous enough to surprise us all. He said, "People *die* in bed!"

People die anywhere you might happen to go, and if you go there, you are increasing the risk of being one of the people who die there. Perhaps you, or perhaps the other guy.

A healthy society is one which is prudent and cautious with regard to unacceptable risks, and which simultaneously has a robust and welcoming stance toward natural and healthy risk. A mother who prevents her son from doing anything "where he might get hurt" is damaging him in all kinds of ways where it is hard to identify the source of the bleeding.

Now as we will see in the next chapter, pot smoking presents identifiable and significant risks to society as a whole. The basic question is this: at what point does that society have the right to outlaw pot smoking as a defensive measure, without that defensive action being in any way a tyrannical overreach?

If one pothead in twenty-five is going to have a murderous psychotic episode, is *that* the line? One in five? One in a thousand?

The biblical principle to apply here is the one found in the laws concerning the quarantine of lepers:

> *The leper in whom the plague is, his clothes shall be rent, and his head bare, and he shall put a covering upon his upper lip, and shall cry, Unclean, unclean. All the days wherein the plague shall be in him he shall be defiled; he is unclean: he shall dwell alone; without the camp shall his habitation be. (Lev. 13:45–46)*

This is a contagious disease, and it is not tyrannical at all for that society to isolate such a man, even if he had read certain articles on the internet that persuaded *him* that he was not contagious at all. When it comes to contagious diseases, *that is not a question for him to decide.* At some point, the society has the authority to decide what is acceptable risk and what is not. They, after all, are the ones being exposed to the risk.

Note that it is not necessary to prove that the infected person will in fact spread the disease to 100 percent of the people he comes into contact with. What is important is that he is contagious—not that he is *inexorably* contagious.

Now, we don't quarantine people with the common cold, because surrendering our rights of free movement on the off chance of preventing the mere nuisance of a cold to others is not a worthwhile exchange. But whooping cough is another matter. Leprosy, at least for God and Moses, was also another matter.

One of the reasons why we want to be governed by wise, prudential men is because Scripture does not give us exact ratios by which to measure whether or not a risk is acceptable. We are never told that if the chances are one in twenty-five that someone will lose their life, it is permissible to ban that activity. Wisdom doesn't work that way. And wisdom has to take all kinds of variables into account.

One of the variables that has to be weighed in the balance is the variable of special pleading. In other words, when it comes to our lusts, the human race really is self-delusional. We are *likely* to believe that gambling, porn, pot-smoking, and the like are "victimless" crimes, which means that, according to this kind of calculation, they ought not to be crimes at all.

But victims bleed out in different ways. They can do this and still be victims. And so society can be harmed also, in tangible ways, and numerous victims within that society can be harmed as well. We might agree on the principle, but when it comes to smoking pot, it has to be said that we are very much in denial.

TAKEAWAY #7: THE CORRELATION BETWEEN MARIJUANA AND VIOLENT PSYCHOSIS REQUIRES CAREFUL, UNBIASED STUDY BEFORE WE REVAMP OUR MARIJUANA LAWS.

CHAPTER EIGHT

JOINTS VERSUS CIGARETTES AS ACTUAL HAZARDS

In what might perhaps be classed as a guilty pleasure, I have followed the comic strip *Doonesbury* for decades. The creator, Gary Trudeau, unlike many on the left, has an actual sense of humor. But we can tell he is a true liberal in that his sense of humor does tend to evaporate, along with his usual sense of proportion (the sense upon which all true humor depends), when he gets himself enmeshed in certain topics. That topic might be the current Republican president, whoever it is this time, or it might be his fascination with tobacco and pot.

Since we are not here to talk about Republican presidents, I want to focus for a moment on Trudeau's strange myopia when it comes to two things that can be lit on fire and smoked—tobacco and cannabis.

Zonker Harris is one of his beloved characters, a stoner from the earliest days, and who is now a marijuana farmer, spreading goodness and cheer in every direction. He is affable, funny, and one from whom the ethos of the entire Doonesbury world radiates. In a stark contrast, Mr. Butts (another character who is a very tall, walking and talking cigarette) is the personification of the grasping and cynical tobacco industry, operating as it does with a callous disregard for human lives, placing profits over the health of men, women, and children.

Now I do not mind critical attacks on the tobacco industry, not at all, but attacks fueled by high hypocrisy are going to come back and bite someone. One of the lines taken in exposing Mr. Butts is the argument that the tobacco industry moguls *knew* that tobacco was bad for the customer, and they tried to expand their markets anyway. If someone takes up smoking as a teenager, in response to some sexy ad, and if fifty years later that same person is dying of lung cancer in a retirement center somewhere, then should not some of those executives who sponsored that initial ad campaign be called upon to answer for their behavior? I mean, what did the evil ad execs know, and when did they know it?

But some cautionary words might be uttered at this point.

> *Judge not, that you be not judged. For with what judgment you judge, you will be judged; and with the measure you use, it will be measured back to you. (Matthew 7:1–2, NKJV)*

What this means is that the level of information that condemns the tobacco-mongers is the same level of information that will condemn the marijuana-mongers in the future, along with their fanboy Gary Trudeau. What did those arguing for legalized marijuana know, and when did they know it? Gogek says, "A critical factor that didn't exist in the 1970s is today's advanced research on marijuana."[7]

A *lot* of research has been done on the effects of marijuana over the last generation, and we now know that it brings far more with it than simply a benign buzz: "Since marijuana has permanent effects on the teenage brain even when used only a few times, all adolescent use is probably abuse."[8]

Among the advocates of legal marijuana, there seems to be a singular lack of curiosity about the effects this drug might have on the demographic category most prone to trying something in pursuit of kicks.

> *"Teenagers get addicted to drugs—including alcohol, marijuana, and tobacco—much more frequently than adults do because their brains are*

7. Gogek, kindle loc. 234.
8. Gogek, kindle loc. 133.

> shaping themselves around their daily experi-
> ences and strengthening the synapses of activities
> they're engaged in. If a teenager is using drugs, the
> parts of the brain that enjoy getting high will be
> strengthened—permanently.[9]

Not only are the effects negative, but the impact of marijuana is far more *serious* than the effects of tobacco. Would you rather die of emphysema fifty years from now or in a psych ward in your late twenties? I would rather have tar in my lungs than tar in my ability to think.

> This research shows that the age at which people
> start using matters. People who use marijuana
> before age seventeen or eighteen can inflict per-
> manent damage. And most marijuana users start
> before age eighteen.[10]

This kind of thing is common sense. People were calling cigarettes "coffin nails" long before the surgeon general insisted that warnings be placed on cartons of cigarettes. In the same way, and using the same kind of common sense, pot users have a reputation for being sky pilots *for a reason.*

> The research on heavy teenage use is overwhelm-
> ingly clear: heavy marijuana use in teenagers per-
> manently alters the ability to think, remember,
> and process.[11]

9. Gogek, kindle loc. 376.
10. Gogek, kindle loc. 415.
11. Gogek, kindle loc. 508.

This is actually something Trudeau knows full well, because Zonker Harris is the quintessential sky pilot. He is Cheech and Chong rolled into one, and yet in the hands of Trudeau, he is still drawn as a lovable character. He is one of the characters in the know, one of the characters who can break the fourth wall and speak to the readers as a self-aware character from a cartoon strip.

Gogek says, "The alcohol and tobacco industries already target black neighborhoods with advertising; a legal marijuana industry would only exploit them more."[12]

Trudeau doesn't like big corporations that cater to the vices of the poor and downtrodden. So what does he think will happen post-legalization? That the marijuana industry will remain a small ma and pa operation?

And then there is the *indirect* damage that marijuana does. Direct damage would be something like the drug itself causing or inflaming schizophrenia. Indirect damage looks like the same kind of thing as the indirect damage that drunkenness causes—not surprisingly.

> *Marijuana does not kill by overdose, but it is deadly behind the wheel.*[13]

> *12 percent of all fatal traffic accidents involved drivers who tested positive for marijuana.*[14]

12. Gogek, kindle loc. 1563.
13. Gogek, kindle loc. 2829.
14. Gogek, kindle loc. 2830.

A simple question should be posed to champions of marijuana and advocates of its legalization: should the legalization of pot mean that it should be legal for airline pilots to fly while loaded? Or for crane operators to do so? Brain surgeons? In other words, does the condition of being stoned impair judgment and affect reflexes? If it does not, then there is no reason why your next Delta pilot might not be high in *two* ways. But if it does impair in this way, then why on earth should we want people in this condition out on the freeway?

> *A review by Columbia University researchers of more than 20,000 fatal accidents found that the percentage caused by marijuana tripled in the first decade of this century*[15]

But because we are talking about a partisan political issue now, and not a dispassionate public health issue, there is always a comeback.

Gogek says, "Then facts about stoned drivers causing fatal car wrecks came out, so many advocates switched to claiming pot never killed anyone—by overdose."[16]

In other words, marijuana is not lethal the way some other drugs are—where you can take too much and die that way and for that reason. Let us grant that you can't OD on pot the same way you can OD on other drugs. But you still have to get home, and the usual way to do so is to get behind the wheel and go. Now can a marijuana-impaired driver on a freeway make the same

15. Gogek, kindle loc. 3269.
16. Gogek, kindle loc. 2877.

kind of mistakes that would make us not want stoners flying commercial airplanes?

And the answer is yes, why, yes they can.

TAKEAWAY #8: WORLDWIDE CRITICISM OF THE TOBACCO INDUSTRY'S HEALTH EFFECTS, MANIPULATION, AND GREED SHOULD BE EQUALLY APPLIED TO MARIJUANA.

CHAPTER NINE

DEEP INCENTIVES

One of the things we need to get straight in our minds is how the world actually works. And by this I am referring to something deeper than mere custom. Midway between the customs of fashion on the one hand (think of something like narrow neckties) and the near universal pattern of nature, which would require a miracle from God to interrupt (like the law of gravity when challenged by Jesus walking on the water), we can on average identify some *necessary* patterns of human nature.

I am here addressing what might be called *deep incentives*. Because it is easier to walk downhill than uphill, a path in the woods is going to be established by hikers over time, and that path is going to take the route of least resistance. The path is going to be developed on the downhill option, and nobody has to ask why. Now this is not an *absolute* necessity, in that it is certainly possible for hikers to go the uphill route. Nobody is stopping them. But we still know how it is going to go.

There are naturally exceptions. It is not the case that human beings will always behave in the ways I am about to describe in the same way that triangles will always have three sides. But at the same time, if someone starts betting against these sorts of things happening, he is going to lose his shirt rapidly and go home from Vegas somewhat discouraged.

What am I talking about? P.J. O'Rourke put it well when he said that "when buying and selling are controlled by legislation, the first things to be bought and sold are legislators." This should be put in the same category as "If you leave your wallet on your dashboard regularly, don't be surprised one day when you find it gone." People who walk by your car don't steal wallets the same way that water runs downhill, but they steal wallets often enough that the practice of wallet exposure is not generally recommended.

So with that said, what happens when an industry that caters to a particular vice is allowed to form and become established? For our purposes here, I am *not* addressing industries where the product is one that has widespread wholesome uses in addition to the uses of vice. The legalization of prostitution is the legalization of vice. The legalization of alcohol is not. I have been arguing that the legalization of pot is in the former category, and not in the latter. Such a legalization will have necessary cultural ramifications.

Again Gogek says, "Once an industry is created, it will influence politicians far more than politicians will influence it."[17]

We have to remember that we are a fallen race and that we sin downhill. We compromise downhill. We grow less disciplined downhill. It is not *hard* to go downhill. Once an industry is created, and the industry caters to vice, the slide is already in motion. There will be more and more demand for the addictive and enervating product. And as that product is sold to more and more customers, the trends are reinforced. The companies selling the vice make more and more money. They hire marketers, lawyers, and lobbyists. Because the product is legal now, the sales are taxed. Those taxes produce new revenue, and for politicians, new revenue is their very own kind of addictive drug.

In short form, there is now a stream of revenue that the civil government has a financial interest to maintain, but that stream of revenue depends upon more and more of the citizenry becoming stoners. Not only so, but the fact that the government is regulating this new pot industry means that the industry is incentivized to hire lobbyists to start chumming around with politicians. Pot lobbyists and your congressman start playing golf together.

17. Gogek, kindle loc. 3530.

You will get more of what you subsidize. You get less of what you penalize. It's true.

You never want a situation to develop where the civil government has become dependent upon the continued corruption of the citizenry. You want a situation where the civil government is dependent upon the *virtue* of the citizenry. But you cannot have that if the citizens have all become lotus eaters. You don't want everyone walking to the polls with a vacant look in their eyes—voting for the candidate that the voices in their head favor.

We have somehow come to believe that we can figure out a way to make a good omelet with rotten eggs. What happens at the individual level is not irrelevant to what happens at the broader societal level. We have tended to assume that society "just is," so if you wreck your life at an individual level, this does not really affect the corporate realities.

But societies, like other bodies, can be afflicted with disease. And societies, like other bodies, can have a collapsed immune system.

A society is an organic body, and like other bodies, it can have a disease that is well contained by the immune system, and it can also have a disease that has overwhelmed the immune system. In other words, societies can have AIDS. If we assume that "normal" society can always function normally, regardless of how many druggies and winos there are, we are presuming far too much. This is like saying that because someone's physical body can fight off five or ten viruses, then it must follow that it can fight off five or ten billion of them.

Certain cultures are industrious, and others are lazy. Some cultures are honest, while others are deceptive. Certain cultures are straitlaced, and others are licentious. That being said, it is possible for a culture with one set of characteristics to be changed into something different.

> *One of themselves, even a prophet of their own, said, the Cretians are alway liars, evil beasts, slow bellies. This witness is true. Wherefore rebuke them sharply, that they may be sound in the faith. (Titus 1:12–13)*

Notice that Paul says that Cretans are a particular way, but notice also that he tells Titus to rebuke them sharply so that they can learn how to be *different*. In other words, he is not fatalistic about it. Cultures can grow in virtue, and cultures can also be corrupted in vice.

With all this said, it is important to remember what law is incapable of doing. When it comes to punishing the wrongdoer, which Scripture tells us is one of the functions of government, we have to remember that this only works around the edges. A law that absolutely everyone disregarded would be a law that was unenforceable. A police department, even a police department that is well-staffed, cannot arrest *everybody*.

> *Knowing this, that the law is not made for a righteous man, but for the lawless and disobedient, for the ungodly and for sinners, for unholy and profane, for murderers of fathers and murderers*

> *of mothers, for manslayers, for whoremongers,*
> *for them that defile themselves with mankind, for*
> *menstealers, for liars, for perjured persons, and if*
> *there be any other thing that is contrary to sound*
> *doctrine. (1 Tim. 1:9–10)*

When a society is largely made up of law-abiding individuals, people who are self-governed, then it is possible for the cops to chase down and deal with the outlaws around the periphery. That *is* possible. And if this is done with sufficient rigor, and the justice of it is apparent, then it does have a deterrent value for those who were thinking of undertaking a crime spree.

> *Because sentence against an evil work is not ex-*
> *ecuted speedily, therefore the heart of the sons of*
> *men is fully set in them to do evil. (Eccles. 8:11)*

When the magistrate knocks heads speedily, it does have a beneficial value. But this is a maintenance value, not a constructive one. The law can help to maintain a moral order, but has no capacity at all when it comes to creating a moral order.

> *For the promise, that he should be the heir of the*
> *world, was not to Abraham, or to his seed, through*
> *the law, but through the righteousness of faith.*
> *(Rom. 4:13)*

Abraham was promised the world, but this world was not going to be given to him "through the law." The most enlightened legal system in the cosmos is unworkable if nobody intends to obey it. As just observed, you cannot arrest everyone.

The overwhelming majority of the population needs to be self-governing. Outliers can be dealt with, but when everyone is an outlier, then the situation becomes impossible.

When the gospel is preached freely and widely in a culture, evangelism is generally successful, and the people consider themselves Christian, then laws can guard the perimeter. But when the laws must guard everything, then everything is insecure.

Imagine that you have a population of 1,000 people, and that one of them is a drug addict. He steals to support his habit, and he buys his drugs from a dealer in the next town over, a place with 5,000 people and 10 addicts. The first town is going to be capable of "carrying" this problem case. He gets periodically arrested, either for possession or for theft, but life in that town is not generally disrupted. Now suppose that 250 people out of the 1,000 have the same problem. Now what? That is *not* sustainable, even though the crimes are all the same— petty theft and drug use. Put another way, an increase in quantity can cause qualitative problems at some point.

And to conclude this chapter with the central thought, the task of righteous law is two-fold. The first is to police the outliers, and the second is to prevent such outlying from going mainstream. Because when that happens, society is officially on life-support.

TAKEAWAY #9: LEGALIZING MARIJUANA WILL HAVE THE EFFECT OF INCENTIVIZING VICE, MOVING OUR CULTURE EVEN FURTHER FROM CAPABLE SELF-GOVERNANCE.

CHAPTER TEN

DRUG COURTS

So what are we supposed to *do* about all of this? Given that a society has the right to defend itself from drug abusers, to the extent that such abusers actually threaten society, and also given the fact that it seems entirely disproportionate to treat a man with an addiction as though he were a violent felon, what are we supposed to do?

Suppose I persuaded everyone that the legalization of pot is a bad idea, but I also agreed with them that our current system is not all that hot either. Remember that sound laws will only work if the people are by and large self-disciplined. That said, what would I propose instead?

In the discussion that follows, I am limiting myself to what should be done about a case of *mere possession*. Say a twenty-year-old man has been arrested with a bag of pot. What should we do with him? I am not talking about what should be done when the Coast Guard catches a drug-running submarine. That would be a discussion for another time.

I am here proposing that mere possession be *decriminalized*, but decriminalized in its own special category. Nobody should do hard time in the penitentiary for lighting up a joint. At the same time, because society should continue to formally disapprove of such drug use, we need to have a mechanism that registers this disapproval in a proportionate way.

But whatever the level of prohibition, that level must have some teeth. This is because parking tickets are also not a criminal offense, and we don't want drug abuse to assume the same status as parking for four hours in a three-hour zone. That would flatten the difference between drug use and common civil infractions, and that would not be good because your present writer, as the Victorians might put it, has at times been guilty of the latter. And if he has been guilty of the latter, and we flatten these offenses into the same kind of offense, it would reduce his moral authority in his effort to write a book like this one. And that would be bad.

So this means that when someone is caught with illegal drugs, he would go to *drug court*. Such drug courts would have a small array of penalties available to him, and if found guilty, the defendant would be given the option of choosing what happens to him. These alternative penalties would be either a fine (rated according to how many drug convictions the defendant has had), or successful completion of a drug treatment program.

Let me illustrate this with arbitrarily chosen numbers. On a first conviction, the fine would be a thousand dollars. The second conviction would be five thousand dollars. The third conviction would be ten thousand dollars. Each time the defendant would be given the option of enrolling in a drug treatment program instead of paying the fine. If he went to rehab and completed the course, then there would be no fine owed. If he was kicked out of the program, or otherwise failed to complete it, then he would owe the fine.

At the same time, while mere possession will have been decriminalized, a refusal or failure to pay such fines would *not* have been decriminalized. In other words, say someone was arrested on a misdemeanor charge for drug possession and was given the option of going through rehab. This is not a disproportionate response at all. The only person who is capable of ratcheting up his offense to a felony would be the defendant himself. If he ran afoul of the courts for not paying his fine, he could well find himself with a serious charge against him. But it would not be a *drug* charge, and he would not be hammered by the state for having had an addiction.

Now by the time we were prepared to do anything so sensible as this, we would have long gotten over our separation of church and state skittishness, which means that the drug court could also allow the defendant to select an explicitly Christian rehab center, which offer treatment programs that are more effective anyhow.

The costs of the treatment program would be borne by the person going through the program (or by his family or friends). In addition, the private Christian programs would almost certainly have scholarships available through mercy ministry programs of local churches.

For those convicted who opt to pay the fine rather than go to treatment, those monies would go into a scholarship fund available for individuals who want to go through treatment but can't afford it for various reasons.

Now, going through treatment does assume addiction on the part of the person convicted of possession, which would not always be the case. But it would be the case often enough to justify the assumption. And for such non-addicted people, rehab should be a snap. If you are not addicted to anything, then it should be pretty easy to go cold turkey. A virulent objection to *any* need for rehab is most likely to come from those who are in the greatest need of rehab.

So in my ideal set-up, the treatment programs would *not* be run by the state, but would instead be private programs that the state would refer people to if they opted not to pay the fine. The job of the magistrate is to make it safe for citizens to walk around on the streets at night; it is not to fix the hearts and souls of people who have addiction issues. The magistrate's job is to keep people off the streets while in that (dangerous) condition.

As the list of treatment centers is offered to the defendants, the drug court would take care to rank the treatment centers, with the number-one ranked center having the smallest percentage of its alumni showing up back in drug court for a subsequent drug offense. The most effective treatment centers would be evaluated by the court on the basis of how much good they actually do in the real world, and not on the basis of any abstract bureaucratic criteria.

As such a system is set up, care would have to be taken so that perverse incentives would not kick in. Actually, I have to qualify that, because perverse incentives *always* kick in. Someone will always figure out a way of feathering his own nest, whatever we do. At the same time, we should look to minimize that kind of thing, as much as possible.

So this approach is not a war on drugs. This is not a case of the civil magistrate undertaking to go out there in order to make all people sober and virtuous. That is not the magistrate's job, and they would be no good at it, even if it were their job. Only the Spirit of God can make people sober and virtuous. The civil magistrate's job is to make the people act, in public, *as though* they were virtuous.

As argued earlier, this is simply a shield that society would use to defend itself against drug abusers, and society would be doing so in a manner that would be calculated not to provoke a reaction against it. Those who want drugs to be legal have not hesitated to highlight any such miscarriages of justice—where some guy was sent up the river for years for possession of three ounces of marijuana. It is important that society's response to the actual threat that drug users pose not be a disproportionate response.

The role of the magistrate is assigned to him by God, and it is not the role of savior. Only Christ is Savior. Our current criminal justice system grew out of attempts on the part of the magistrate to make men good. Just consider the terminology. Why do we send men to penitentiaries? The answer would appear to be so that they might become *penitents*. Why do we send troubled young people to reformatories? So that they might *reform*. But what actually happens is that these institutions become graduate schools for the inculcation of vice.

There should be a way for society to take a stand against the very real threat that drug abusers pose, while at the same time not hardening them into permanent drug abusers. This proposal, or something very much like it, would have sufficient teeth to work—having to spend a couple of months in rehab would be a serious dislocation for most people. At the same time, it would not be time thrown down a rat hole. There would be long-term benefits *for the defendant*. Clean and sober gets and keeps the job.

So the drug courts would be interested in achieving one basic result: not to see the same defendant multiple times, charged with the same offense. This process would not necessarily make the defendant a good person (although it might). What the drug court is trying to do is make the defendant relatively harmless to society.

And that should be sufficient.

TAKEAWAY #10: JUSTICE REQUIRES THAT DRUG ENFORCEMENT LAWS "HAVE TEETH" WITHOUT BEING DRACONIAN. OUR SYSTEM COULD BE MUCH REFORMED.

MERE GOSPEL

Apart from the transforming power of the gospel, men and women *want* to sin. They want to sin individually, and they want to sin in groups. The reason they want to do so is that, in the short run, it is fun: "There is a way which seemeth right unto a man, but the end thereof are the ways of death" (Prov. 14:12; 16:25).

And so it seems like a good idea at the beginning, but later, when the bills start to come due, a different kind of calculation can commend itself. The prodigal son, staring at the pig food, came to a different frame of mind than he had when he was still able to buy drinks for all the girls (Luke 15:16–17).

The one who rejects the warnings about loose women in Proverbs comes to regret it later: "And say, How have I hated instruction, and my heart despised reproof" (Prov. 5:12).

But when he comes to this point, he does not need to turn over a new leaf. He needs new life, not a new leaf. He needs to cry out in true repentance, and ask for God's mercy.

Now what happens when a man is converted in this way is that he is given the power of new *life*. He is not given, in the first instance, a new set of *rules*. When biblical morality is clamped on from outside, it only provokes revolt. This is true of individuals, and it is true of cultures.

But the impact of real conversion is the same with groups, with societies, with cultures. When a number of people are converted to God, and there has been a real heart change, their behavior, along with their cultural norms and expectations, change right along with them.

As time passes, however, the wineskins get old and cracked. The institutional morality, inherited from the living past, seems like it is not alive anymore. That is because it is not. When the faith of the people dies, the things that depended on that faith will also die.

If there is a great reformation among the people, their laws and customs will come to reflect that. But those laws and customs might well outlive the faith of the ones who generated those customs. The dead weight of those expectations will be felt *as* dead weight by the unregenerate heirs of the tradition.

Henry van Til once observed that culture is religion externalized. This is quite true. But it is also true that culture can be diseased religion externalized, and culture can also be apostasy externalized. Culture is the spiritual state of the people externalized.

And so this goes in both directions—reformations and deformations both. So, by the same token, when a society has enjoyed a season of spiritual refreshing, the culture that takes shape around it will be a vibrant culture. When society collapses into narcissistic self-absorption, it will not be long before porn is everywhere, sodomy is celebrated, and smoking pot seems like just the thing that everybody needs to start doing.

People want to smoke pot because it feels good. And if a lot of people take it up, then a lot of people feel good, at least for the time being. Not only so, but there appears to be no good reason for them to abstain. The only people who want them to abstain are the killjoys, right? As believers, we have to recognize that when Christ is absent, such reasoning makes perfect sense. If the dead do not rise, let us eat, drink, *smoke whatever*, and be merry, for tomorrow we die (1 Cor 15:32).

But it is important not to make a fatal mistake at this point. Christ is Lord, and if we acknowledge His lordship, it is true that the new life He grants will have the result of getting us clean and sober. That will happen. Once converted to God, we walk in newness of life. But we must not approach Him as though He were some sort of patent medicine. His authority must be accepted on its own terms. He is Lord, and must be acknowledged as Lord for that reason only.

We are invited to turn to God through Christ because He died on the cross for our sins and was raised to life for our justification (Rom. 4:25). If we come to Him, it must be because we believe that this account is true. We must believe that He actually did die, and that He actually did come back from the grave. If we believe that, for that reason, everything will fall into place. But if we use His name as an incantation for the sake of our highest value, which is getting things to fall into place, then nothing will. Everything will continue to fall apart.

If we treat Christ as the means to an end (freedom from drugs, say), then we are not coming to Him as Christ. He is a Savior, not a self-help specialist. We come to the Giver for who He is and not for the gifts that He might give. At the same time, He *is* the Giver of gifts (Eph. 4:8).

When the prodigal son repented, part of what enabled him to see his true condition was the food that he wanted to eat as compared with the food and clothing that his father's servants had back home. But at the same time, he knew that he could not return home, acting as though his father were nothing more than an animate vending machine. *That* was how he had treated him the first time.

So it is not as though the "condition our condition is in" has nothing to do with it. We are creatures with nerve endings, and God can speak to us through them. There are different analogies to help us navigate this. Our need for Him should be a window through which we look in order to see Him. We should have one eye on Christ Himself, and the other eye on our desperate condition.

All of this is to say that America will not be clean and sober again apart from Christ. If we value that sobriety *more* than Christ, we will continue to be entrapped in our downward spiral of dissolution. But if we forget the fact that we are lost in our pleasures, then we will not know that we are in need of salvation. That would be bad also.

So Christ is Lord, and we must come to Him as an act of obedience. When we come to Him, it must be with the recognition that He is going to take away our cannabis.

And good riddance.